Still Growing

Kiley Lopez

Presentation by *BookLeaf Publishing*

Web: www.bookleafpub.com

E-mail: info@bookleafpub.com

ISBN: 9789395969239

First edition 2022

Biggest dream

My biggest dream,
is to be free.
Like the birds that
like to sing or
the leaf that
flys in the wind.
I want to be like them.
I want to fly
and I want to soar.
In my biggest dream,
I am free.
Free like never before.

Trying

I'm trying my best.
Even when it's hard.
Even when i'm alone.
I still try.
Please be patient with me.
I'm not lazy.
I'm not rude.
I'm exhausted.
I'm doing the best I can.

Approval

3

You don't need anybody's approval.
It's your life
It's your dream.
Live the best like you can.
You only have one chance.

Relax

Nature is my escape.
Where i'm able to relax
and feel safe.
Where I can go
to clear my mind
and feel like I can breathe.

Anger

5

There is so much anger
that I feel inside of me
and I just want to scream
to let it all out.
I want it to leave.
Like everyone else.

Favorite Season

Winter is my favorite season
The cold
The snow
The quiet
The beauty
Something about it,
is so peaceful.
It makes me feel safe.

Gone

I feel so invisible
Like i'm not here.
No one sees me.
I'm just gone.

Drowning

This depression swallows me whole.
It drowns me.
I'm screaming for help,
but no one hears me.
Or maybe they don't want to.
I'm drowning.
I'm drowning.

Still Growing

9

I'm still growing.
I'm still learning.
I make mistakes,
We all do.
I'm only human.

Surviving

I'm tired of surviving.
I don't mean that I want to die.
I just want to actually live.
One day,
I hope that I don't hate existing.

Meeting You

Meeting you was like a breath of fresh air.
Within you, I found my home.
Somewhere that I felt safe.
You saved me.
You're the light
in a sea of darkness.
From the bottom of my heart,
Thank you.

Dear Mom

Dear Mom,
I know I don't say this a lot but,
i'm proud of you.
I aspire to be as brave
and strong as you.
You are my hero.
Dear Mom,
You're beautiful.
You are doing amazing.

On Repeat

13

I feel like a record
that's on repeat.
Reliving the same day.
Over and over.
It's tiring.
I'm tired of being stuck on replay.

Loner

I've never really ever
had much friends.
I'm a loner.
Everyone always leaves.
I think that maybe
there's just something wrong with me
that scares people away.

Fell In Love

15

We might be young,
but I truly and deeply
fell in love with you.
You were the person who
has shown me patience
and kindness.
You will always be in my heart.
I will forever cherish you.

Liberosis

Liberosis;
the desire to care less about things.
I wish
that I didn't care so much.
In the end,
it always gets me hurt.
I want to care.
But I want to stop caring too much.

Your Actions

17

You say you love me
But it's your actions that
speak louder.

Long Distance

I know we're not
next to each other.
However, i'm lucky enough
to be able to be under the same
sky as you.
I'm grateful that we get to
be under
the same moonlight.
I can't wait until
i'm able to kiss you under it.

Believe

You're strong.
You're powerful.
You're brave.
You can get through it,
even when it feels impossible.
Believe in yourself.

My Best Friend

My best friend,
you have stuck by my side
through my worst
and my best.
You love me
even when I can't
love myself.
There is no way I could ever
repay you.

Dissociation

21

I feel like i'm
disconnected from myself.
Like i'm outside of my body
looking down on myself.
I don't feel
connected with my thoughts
or with myself.
I'm dissociated.

www.ingramcontent.com/pod-product-compliance
Lightning Source LLC
Chambersburg PA
CBHW061330140726
47998CB00007B/2637